"Hello, Somebody!" Beverly Steele's 40 Acres & A Mule Stories. Her people kept the land!

Foreword by Dr. Donald Paul Wyman

ISBN: 9781097189540

Royal Florida

This map is of the Community of Royal today as completed by Digital Heritage Interactive for the Community of Royal, Cultural Resources Assessment Survey in 2017 and adopted by the Sumter County Board of Commissioners in 2015. This Report will be used to help identify Royal as a Historical Site.

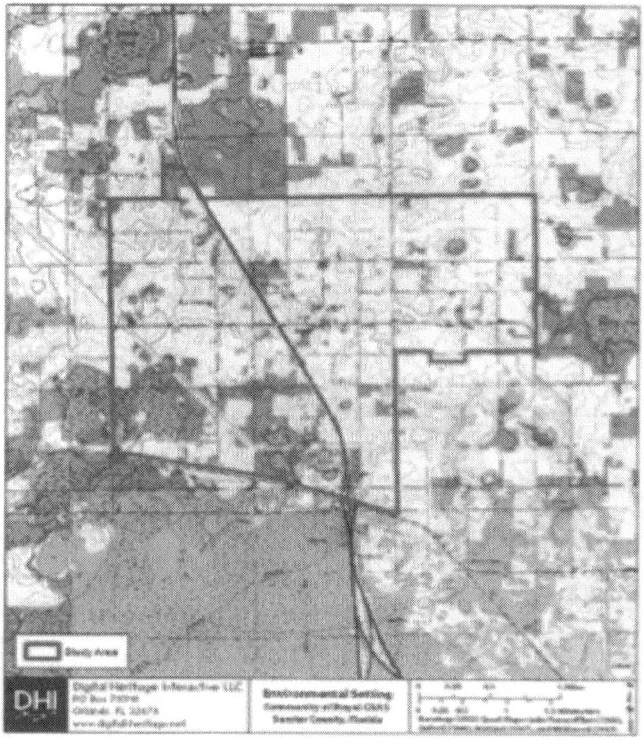

Community of Royal CRAS

DHI

Study Area

Environmental Setting

Figure 1.4: Environmental setting of project study area

May 2017 Digital Heritage Interactive, LLC 5

Foreword

Dr. Donald Paul Wyman

Author of: "The Chosen Path: Based on the Life of Elizabeth Van Lew"

In 1863, on Sherman's "March to the Sea," his army had grown to over 10,000 runaway or former slaves. After the war, they became a major problem. Sherman along with Secretary of War Edwin Stanton met with slave community leaders to get their ideas on how they could best take care of themselves. The slave community leaders explained that they wanted land to farm to take care of their families.

As a result, Special Field Order No. 15 issued January 1865 provided for 400,000 acres in South Carolina, Georgia and Florida to be confiscated and given to the freed slave families to live on. The Freedmen Bureau issued Circular No.13 in July 1865 to provide 40 acres to each slave family and possibly a mule. However, no mules were ever given out.

Sometimes the plantation owners like Master Green (Steele's ancestor's plantation master) directed the freed slaves from the Green Plantation to other plantation land for living and working. On Green's Plantation land, the freed slaves divided up the land into 40 acres with white picket sticks. It became known as "Picketsville" as a result of all the white pickets showing the parceled-out land.

After President Lincoln's assassination, a new Circular No. 15 ordered by President Johnson, revoked the original, and took back the land. Special Field Order No. 15 and Circular No. 13 had provided for over 40,000 freedmen to farm the lands. But now, with the newly enacted Circular No. 15, only 1565 were able to keep it. Steele's people kept their land.

President Johnson supported former slaves becoming sharecroppers and paying the original owners for the use of the land after the crops were harvested. The original owners, who were still feeling both their losses from the Civil War, coupled with both their resentment of losing to the North, were now incensed at being directed to give their former slaves their land or to share their profits. Most original owners did not agree with this humiliating obligation.

By the 1880's and 1890's, the land was considered Public Domain and the freedmen could make land claims. 153 years later, Steele's beloved ancestor's and beloved historic Community of Royal are able to exist and thrive today.

According to state records, the original founding families were the Harleys, the Picketts and the Andersons (Steele's family) that established this historic Community of Royal.

It's educational and inspiring to observe Beverly Steele in action. These capsules from Steele's life story should help us to rekindle the Country's and our own awareness of how far we've come - and how far we have yet to go.

Thank you, Beverly Steele, for sharing these illustrious stories and for being an inspiration to so many young performing artist whose talents the Country will enjoy for many years to come.

"Hello, Somebody!"

Introduction

reprinted from Community of Royal Cultural Resources (CRAS) Assessment Survey by Digital Heritage Interactive June 30, 2017

The community of Royal is part of a much broader history of people of African descent in the state of Florida. The following pages ....provides an introductory history of Royal itself, drawn from the work of local historians and community activists like Beverly Steele......and we provide additional information for contextualizing the results of this CRAS.

Peoples of African descent have been an integral part of Florida's history since the first European explorers visited the area. Free Africans were crew members - often vital ones - who assisted early explorers like Pedro Menéndez de Avilés and Hernando de Soto.

Peoples of African descent have been a part of Florida's history since the initial discovery of the lands referred to by the Spanish as La Florida.

While many of these expeditions proved disastrous for their leaders, numerous persons of African descent escaped during the first half of the 1500s, learned native customs and languages, and remained in Florida for years (Rivers 2000:1-2; Landers 2000, 2013).

Royal is a unique African American community formed in the late 1800s in Sumter County, Florida. While a handful of similar sites were founded during this time, few have survived to the present. Similar rural African American towns, such as Rosewood and Santos were either directly destroyed through racial violence or displaced through development. As such, Royal is one of the most compelling examples of a rural, historically African American town found anywhere in the state of Florida, if not the nation.

Why has Royal survived when other communities did not? There are numerous potential answers to this question. Primary among them is the community that lives in Royal today. Throughout the 20th century it became increasingly difficult for African Americans to live in rural locations throughout the state.

The perseverance of those who live in Royal is a central reason it has survived into the 21st century. Efforts to commemorate this history, by individuals like Beverly Steele and organizations like Young Performing Artists (YPAs) Inc. also play a significant role. Educating the next generation is crucial to understanding the uniqueness of places like Royal.

Another reason Royal has survived may be a result of geography. Rosewood and Santos were both located along railroads, and were the location of train deports. The railroad never arrived in Royal. While this caused the residents inconvenience when hauling their agricultural products to market, it may have also served to insulate the town. Although the area around Royal is good agricultural land, its geophysical characteristics do require considerable effort to maintain throughout the year.

As such, the combination of geography and geology surely played a significant role in protecting the community from destruction and development.

Today, Royal faces new challenges. As with African American communities across the state, economic pressures continue to draw young generations towards the cities.

Developers have also begun to push into the areas and communities around Royal. This includes new housing developments to the east and energy corridors and transportations projects along the southern and western boundaries. With the possible exception of I-75, these threats have not directly impacted the community, although that is likely to change if efforts are not taken to commemorate and preserve some aspect of Royal's cultural and historical integrity.

It is our opinion that Royal represents a nationally significant place regarding African American history. Royal was never incorporated, but neither were many other early communities in Sumter County (e.g., Adamsville). Historical records document the arrival of African Americans during Reconstruction, with land grants being awarded to early black settlers in the 1770s and 1780s.

Oral histories with elderly informants in recent decades suggest the potential that many of these early residents interacted with free African Americans who arrived in previous decades. Historical documents and archaeological evidence already notes the existence of free Blacks in the area during the 1830s. These groups lived relatively close to Royal, and at a time when a distance of a few miles was still close enough to think of folks as neighbors.

The possibility that early residents of Royal interacted with these earlier black communities is tantalizing. However, without the discovery of specific documentary work, this question will have to rely on archaeological investigations in the area to confirm. Regardless, what is known now still defines a period of significance for Royal stretching backwards from the present to the late 1800s, within a few decades of this fascinating history.

Royal's documentable period of significance begins during Florida's frontier days. In the 1870s the peninsula of the state remained sparsely populated.

This did not change significantly until major railroad travel was established and expanded during the 1880s and 1890s.

Royal was occupied by African Americans during both of these times. The 20th century was a time of turmoil and disenfranchisement of African Americans across the state of Florida, and yet Royal persisted. The late 20th century has seen much of this reverse, and African American entering local and state governments.

The first African American to hold office in the government of Sumter County was Robert "Tom" Dixon. He was elected as a County Commissioner of District 1 in 1984. He was a resident of Royal.

The history of Royal, and the architectural evidence standing today, offers a thread connecting all of these times. The concrete tobacco barns are unique resources, with similar examples existing in South Carolina, where they date as early as 1925 (Ingram 2015).

In Royal, the offer a direct connection to local tobacco production in the 19th and 20th centuries. The sugar cane processing facilities in Royal are a key representative aspect of frontier life often associated with Florida, one which has continued right up to the present day.

Numerous community structures have not survived, but are recorded in historical documents. This includes churches, schools, and government buildings. The post office was established in 1891 (Bradbury and Hallock 1891, at the same time as many of the surrounding white communities. Today, the post office has been relocated to Wildwood.

The structures that do survive offer insights into everyday aspects of African American lives that are not always afforded the attention they deserve. The commercial buildings that still stand in Royal may have served as community centers, where community members met to visit and chat local happenings. The masonic hall may have served a similar purpose as a community center, a secondary function held by many black masonic lodges in the state.

.........future work should explore the possibility of nominating the community of Royal to the National Register of Historic Places. Many of the individual architectural resources in this report may not be eligible on their own, but may be as part of a site or district. We specifically encourage future research to concentrate on registering Royal as Rural Historic Landscape.

In closing, the community of Royal offers a unique and fascinating example of African American life in Florida. It is representative of agricultural trends beginning during the frontier times of the state's history and extending into the present. Its existence as a black town is also unique, particularly in light of the fact that similar towns elsewhere in the state have not survived to the present, or have been greatly altered through violence or development. We recommend that future work explore the potential of archaeology to uncover additional data, utility of oral testimony, and prepare a national register nomination as a RHL or site.

"Hello, Somebody!"
An Ancestor's Wake Up Call...

Story 1.

Throughout this book, Steele uses the basic language of her people to convey their stories. This story gets the reader's mind in a 'call to action' mood. Prayerfully, bringing together people who share inspiration from the stories of her ancestor's past to evoke social action.

A funny story, where everyone would laugh, was about "Old Man Earl Haggins." Old Man Haggins worked on the farm for my Big Papa. He was a loner; someone who just walked into the community, looking for work. My Big Papa always helped and hired them. My Big Papa was a great businessman; this is why I named my business in his honor.

Old Man Haggins didn't have a wife; he had a room that he lived. About 5am, every morning he would walk up to Big Papa and Big Mama's house, ready to work and ready for breakfast. The story goes that the houses were made of wood, had gaps between the planks and you could hear everything from the outside.

Old Man Haggins would come a walkin' and he would yell, "Hello, Somebody!" That meant get up, get up; I'm ready to eat and work. It was a wake-up call; a call to action. The Millennials would say, he was 'woke'. Today, we can use a few more Old Man Haggins.

My people, who kept their 40 acres from the Civil War and a mule, were hard working like Old Man Haggins. They said that the women would walk to Oxford, a neighboring white town, to work for pennies a day and sometimes they would get a chicken. They washed clothes, ironed, cooked, cleaned houses and looked after the children. Oxford was 5 miles North of our Royal. Sometimes, my people would carry their babies, on their hips, to work. They would work hard, walk back 5 miles to Royal, carry the baby and maybe a chicken.

Also, Oxford was the place where they took my people to hang. They were told "don't go to Oxford for nothing and if you must go---get out of there as fast as you can". They would tell that story and laugh.

Therefore, my Big Papa hired Old Man Haggins and others because he wanted to help them maintain their sense of freedom. Even though my Big Papa couldn't spare the money, because they had 9 children- 7 girls and 2 boys. He felt he had to hire in order to spare others from enslavement, once again.

Old Man Haggins' "Hello, Somebody!" was a true call to action. Maybe, it meant get up, it's time to work, maintain your freedom and my mine. Learning and hearing of Old Man Haggins' call had a profound affect in my life; thus, the title of this book.

One of the times before acquiring one of my company's contract, I can recall when I challenged a client to 'wake up.' Whenever, I did or do this; it was and is startling. I never understood where I got the nerves nor the fortitude to 'go there' before or even after signing a contract. At that time, contracts were few and far between especially for Women owned consulting firms and almost, non-existence for African American Women owned consulting firms.

It was 1991, my firm was invited to pitch for a contract providing Equity & Diversity marketing initiatives to the Advertising Industry. The industry had a 'dirty little secret'; there were less than 1% minority employees. The industry was feeling the effects of a less diversified industry and this was affecting how they serviced their client's needs.

We proposed an internship program entitled **M**inorities In **A**dvertising **P**rogram with the acronyms of MAP. Mapping a future for the workforce and the industry. The program was opened to all minorities i.e Women, Hispanics, African Americans, etc.

All, but one of the decision makers, was shaking their heads in agreement. All, but one, sat alert and attentive; awaiting a time to speak in agreement. The one waited for a quiet moment, leaned forward and stated "Interns? We need qualified people, now." I, too, leaned forward and stated, "Sir, there are no qualified ones because you haven't hired one to become qualified. Yes. You need interns." He leaned back in his chair.

I finished with "I'm not here to fail; I'm not here for your companies to fail and I, certainly, am not here to place ones in your companies to fail."

At that moment, the intended 'wake up' message was I wanted everyone in that room to know that I began my business to achieve success as any other firm. As well as, I wanted them to take responsibility for the position they had placed their companies and not transfer the blame. Don't transfer the blame to the 'interns placed' nor to the firm placing the interns. The contract was signed, the program began, interns placed, and I've heard that it still exists in some form, today.

That One still voted, NO and refused placement of interns. Sometimes, we just refuse to 'wake up'. Most likely because we have different life experiences; we don't realize that we need to 'wake up'.

"Hello, Somebody!" First, we must wake up.

Story 2. It all began with the "40 Acres and a Mule" Civil War Proclamation

---

This story breathes life to the words of General Sherman's Special Field Order #15. It's a true account of how this order, circular 13 and circular 15 affected Steele's ancestors. Despite it all, the people kept their land.

From a young age, probably around 4th grade, I began to hear the stories that were told by my Elders of how my beloved Community Of Royal was formed. They told the story of how after the signing of the Emancipation Proclamation in1863, and at the end of the Civil War in 1865, how slaves from the Old Green Plantation established Royal.

The Old Green Plantation, near the Withlacoochee River, was due west of Royal and the slaves were set free to go yonder. Now that yonder was probably less than desirable land and the "Massa" (Master) may have thought it 'good enough' for my people. Massa might have thought, "they'll never survive there in that thicket." Survived, they did. Now 150+ years later, my people kept the land.

When the war ended in 1865, General Sherman answered the cry of the freedmen's displacement and having nowhere to go. He issued Special Field Order #15 which granted each freedman 40 Acres confiscated during the war and army mule no longer needed for war.

Historical research supports that many took the offer, but few could hold onto the land after President Abraham Lincoln was assassinated. President Andrew Johnson rescinded the order and encouraged the former landowners to reclaim their land. And that they did, but not Massa Green. I believe that he thought, "they'll never survive there in that thicket!" Or, was there another reason?

Let's explore the legacy of my ancestors. They were crafty, swift, courageous, skillful, hardworking, thankful and blessed to not have Massa come back and reclaim this portion of his land. Remember this was in July 1865 and most freedmen took the offer, became landowners of at least 40 Acres, but the land was taken back by September 1865.

For most, they came from being owned to living the life of a slave and owning nothing; from being free and owning something (land); to being free and not owning anything. That's when most became sharecroppers thus establishing a new legacy for future generations.

But not my people, they kept the land. I believe, it was because of their characteristics of being crafty, swift, courageous, skillful, hardworking and they knew how to thank God for this blessing. I believe that when Massa sent his "spies" to check things out; he was told that my people were hard at working the land to support themselves.

Oh yes, he sent his spies. I remember being told that one day Massa's boys came riding through the community creating havoc … you know, "Boys will be boys." They would ride their horses and run the chickens, the cows, the women, the children, etc.; everybody and everything ran. One day, a shot rang out and one of Massa's boys fell and they said it was Old Man Pickett whose shot rang out.

Of course, Massa came looking for Old Man Pickett but couldn't find him; they hid him in one of the big oak trees. They covered him with moss, hoisted his food up and signaled when to come down for anything else. Some of the community men were still working for Massa Green and Old Man Patterson was one. They said that Old Man Patterson was like a flour shifter and telling him, anything, was like pouring sand through that shifter. He couldn't hold anything. If you wanted it told; tell Old Man Patterson … and they would laugh.

One day after the shooting and at Massa Green's place, Old Man Patterson, who didn't know and wanted to, said to the others: "Y'all boys know where Pickett is?" The reason he didn't know, was because they knew he would tell. He couldn't hold anything, "Lawd have mercy!" Well Massa overheard and thought if Old Man Patterson was sure that the others knew, certainly, he must know. That night, Massa went to Old Man Patterson's house and gave him one good whippin'!" Didn't kill him but gave him one good whippin'. Massa never found Old Man Pickett hiding in the trees because Old Man Patterson really didn't know.

They say that the last they heard of Old Man Pickett was when the younger community boys went to work the "mule train" at the Tampa Bay docks. This story continues that the community boys were loading one of the big ships, one looked and spotted Old Man Pickett. The others doubted because no one had seen Pickett in a long time. The others never looked up and stated 'man, Picket be gone a long time; no one knows where Pickett is. Now, get back to work.' As they continued to load, one of the boys acclaimed to the others, "Look! Man. That is Pickett." Finally, the others looked up and said "Pickett, what ya doin' up there?"

According to the boys, Pickett was on the bow of one of the big ships that was backing out of the Bay. He was waving and smiling as if to say, "Hello boys; good to see ya boys; see ya around boys," as the boat sailed away. They would tell that story and laugh.

My people had strong faith and they would laugh even after talking about something bad. They believe in God the Father, Jesus the Son and the Holy Ghost. They believe that God will ne'er forsake you and ne'er leave you alone. If you accept, believe, serve and expect the blessings; He will bless you.

Maybe, one of the other reasons that Massa didn't take the land back was because he knew how hard my people worked on the Plantation. He had witnessed their characteristics of being crafty, swift, courageous, skillful, hardworking and they knew how to thank God for this blessing. I believe that the Community boys continued to work with him because they had garnered a mutual respect.

They kept their land. A Civil War proclamation.

Hello, Somebody!" Mutual respect can garner a greater good.

Story 3. Royal: What's in a name?

Freed Africans resided in Florida before the Civil War. Most were 'Black Seminoles'. Steele tells of how her beloved Royal was inhabited by a settlement of freed Africans before the Civil War. From African Royalty to Royal.

Always, I thought my people freedom story began with the "40 Acres and a Mule" Special Field Order #15 with their newfound land ownership. While researching 'why the name Royal from Pickettsville?', I discovered that my people freedom story didn't begin in 1865. It may have begun in 1848-49. I didn't know because the community residents didn't know. While researching for records to be placed in our new Enrichment & Historical Center, we learned about the Freedman's Bureau and General William Tecumseh Sherman's Special Field Order #15.

As long as I can remember, Royal had a few white families on its western and northern boundaries. One day, one of the families sent me his family's history. Their history was already a published book and he gifted us one for placement in our center.

According to my people, we have always lived like neighbors; they never gave us any trouble and we never gave them any trouble. My people worked for this same family.

My first thought was "why should this book be placed in our center and why should I place it in our center?" So, I thanked them and took it to review its significance to Royal's history and it's placement at our historic center.

After approximately two weeks, I knew that I needed to decide to place or not to place? Plus, I could hear my Big Mama in my ear, saying "I taught you manners. That book was given for our center and you need to remember the manners I taught you and place that book at the center." I was procrastinating but I wanted to get Big Mama out of my ears. "Alright, alright Big Mama, I hear you!", I proclaimed.

I began to flip pages and there were maps of the area (circa early 1800s); I thought that's significant. I flipped more pages and flipped upon two significant pages: one about Mr. George Wideman and the other about Reverend Mathew Beard - both I knew from Royal.

Yes, Mr. George died at an early age, in his 80s, but his wife, Mother Polly Wideman, died at the tender age of 109.

My people say that Reverend Beard wasn't born in Royal, but his family walked into Royal when he was approximately 6 years old. At the tender age of 115, he died. It's rumored that he preached his last sermon on the Sunday before he died. Both are pictured on our 'Wall of Honor' in our center and they're buried in our Community Cemetery, Oak Hill. Now. That's significant; stories about my people.

As I continued to flip the book pages, I found a chapter on Royal. According to this family history, in 1848-49when this family arrived in our area they found a group of freed Africans. The white families co-habituated with the Africans, who taught them how to work the land and how to benefit from the Gum Slough River, a natural aquifer. As it continued, this group of freed Africans were "clean-bloodied" which meant they did not mix blood with Whites nor native Americans nor Europeans.

They were Kings & Queens in Africa and had settled this area naming it Royalsville. They named it Royalsville so that future generations (I, Steele) would know that they were of African Royalty.

It continues, that it became known as Picketsville, then in the late 1890s it was renamed Royal. According to State records, Royal was issued a Post Office in July 1891. From 1848-1891, the names were Royalsville to Picketsville to Royal. What's in a name? Years of blood, sweat and tears.

Now, that's very significant, especially for me. I always knew that my community was special and blessed. But to learn that freed Africans formed it,
before the Civil War, was an eye opener. I never knew that all Africans did not remain enslaved upon arrival in this country. There were some who were freed almost on arrive i.e. Mary Kingsley whom a British Gentleman married thus granting her freedom. Mrs. Kingsley had slaves that serviced her plantation.

And, there were some that walked into Florida, which was Spanish governed, and gained their freedom. The slaves, in Georgia, Alabama and other slave known states, were told that if they could safely walk into Florida, join the Spaniards to help fight the Indians, become Catholic, they would be free. In the bible, Mark 10:45 reads 'so if the Son sets you free, you will be free indeed.' The slaves realized that if they walked into Florida, join the Indians, not become Catholic.... they would be free indeed. Florida did not join the union until the 1820s. Because of this fact, plantations didn't exist in Florida until that time and up until the Civil War.

Remember, I was trying to justify the book's significance to Royal's history and its placement at our historic center. I didn't know this part of our history until after researching the readings of this book. What's in a name? Honor, heritage, knowledge, fulfillment, legacy, determination, courage, thankfulness ... Royalty; Royal.

"Hello, Somebody!" Wake up! Your equity & diversity lesson from this story- don't judge the book by its cover.

Story 4. Who Were My People?

Heritage? What's heritage? As a 4th grader, Steele tells this story of her beloved Royal Community illustrious heritage and history.

Heritage? What's heritage? According to dictionary.com, heritage is something that is handed down from the past, as a tradition: a national heritage of honor, pride, and courage. Is heritage the stories that I heard my Big Mama (Grandma), Aunts, Cousins and other folks talking about the good old days? If it is, then I remember some of those stories of how my Community Of Royal began in 1865.

They said the first people came from the Old Green Plantation west of the community and next to the Withlacoochee River. They said they were slaves and freed because President Lincoln signed the Emancipation Proclamation.

A Florida State archived document lists my Big Mama's family (the Andersons) as one of the first settlers of Royal. They said the Harleys and the Picketts were some of the other first families, who came from the Old Green Plantation, as well.

They said, after President Lincoln signed the Proclamation freeing everyone from slavery and at the end of the Civil War, that General William Sherman signed a special field order #15 giving everyone 40 acres and one of the army mules to homestead and provide for their families.

Therefore, where I live, everyone has 40, 80 and some 120 acres of land. They say this is very rare because after President Lincoln was shot and killed; President Johnson rescinded that special field order #15 and the land was taken from most of my people. Somehow, we kept our land in Royal. I've learned that President Johnson and General Sherman did not see 'eye to eye' regarding the 'Reconstruction'. Those two were like 'oil & water'; did not mix; did not agree. President Johnson striped Sherman of almost all his war medals. Maybe, the President rescinded Special Field Order # 15 because he wanted to get back at Sherman; not my people. Who knows?

They said the people were hard workers, honest and respectful of each other and each other's property. They helped each other with farming and providing food for everyone. They planted corn, tobacco, peas, cotton, greens, tomatoes, sugar cane, sweet potatoes and other stuff. They looked out for everyone and would share food with each other.

They said, when it was time to harvest the sugar cane, the people would gather the sugar cane from everyone's field and come together. It became a sugar cane grinding and cooking sugar cane syrup community day. They would use the sugar cane syrup to sweeten cakes, coffee and tea. My Big Mama was one of the best bakers in the community; she made the best teacakes. A teacake is like a biscuit but sweetened with sugar cane syrup.

They raised hogs, cows, goats and chickens. When they needed sausages, ham, ribs, pig feet, pig tails, pig ears; they would have a "hog killing day" where several families would bring their hogs and they worked together to gather food for their families.

Always, they would big a big fire. My Big Mama would take some of the sweet potatoes from the field and place them in the ashes of the fire so they could slow roast. All the children couldn't wait to eat sweet treats fresh from the field and hot out of the ashes. My Big Mama was the best.

They said some of the other families were the James', the Mathews', the Keilers, the Pattersons, the Seslers, etc. They said the Harleys and the Picketts along with the Andersons (my family) were the first families here. I know there are some of the Harleys who still live here but I didn't know of any of the Picketts until recently. I've learned that the Keilers and Matthews families were a part of the Picketts family via marriage.

My people continued to work hard, serve hard, pray hard and help each other. That's the lesson that our teachers, grandparents, parents, pastors and neighbors taught us: "Do good unto others and others will do good unto you."

My people loved, laughed, cried and served but they always felt safe in this community because they owned the land and were free. In the words of the Reverend Dr. Martin Luther King, Jr.: "Free at last, Free at last. Thank God Almighty, we are free at last." (Lincoln Memorial Speech, August 28, 1963)

"Hello, Somebody!" Wake up to serve.

Story 5. Quilts Will Lead the Way

Steele explains how quilts were sewn so that they helped fugitive slaves travel to freedom.

One more story about my people; I remember that they made everything from pillowcases from feed bags filled with moss to moss filled mattresses to handmade quilts to cover the beds.

Speaking of quilts, my Big Mama would make quilts; some were hand quilted, some tacked with yarn; some intricate patterns; some simple; all depending on why she made that quilt. If a quilt was made as a gift, the quilt could become very intricate. If not, or made for a child's room, those could be very simple. Some of the quilts, she would hold in her lap and stitch. Some, she would roll into a quilter's frame. Some, she would stitch alone and others with her friends/ neighbors.

What interests me, the most, was the patterns. She would sew the monkey wrench, the star, cabin in the ground, bow tie, basket, sail boat, etc. to make the tops.

I, always, wondered why those patterns because most of her friends would use the same patterns. When asked they would simply state, "My Mama or Grandmama used those patterns and taught us."

As I continued to research history for our center, I wanted to include something about Ms. Harriet Tubman and her Underground Railroad.

We were donated a beautiful picture depicting the artists' visual of this great event. That was nice but I wanted something that dug deeper into that magnificent event. One of my consulting firm's clients, where we handled Equity & Diversity initiatives, I was told about an Elderly White Female who made a quilt that someone suggested that we look.

Upon agreeing, I went to look at this quilt that may have some significance to the Underground Railroad. When she pulled out the quilt, which was made up of some of the same symbols that were on my Grandmother's quilts; I became excited. "How do you know about these symbols? What does these symbols mean to you? Did your Grandma quilt? Did she use these symbols?"

She began to share her love of sewing and quilting; she beamed with remembrance of how her Grandmother showed her how to sew and make beautiful things. She loved sewing period things whether clothing, hats and/or quilts. With this love for sewing historic items, someone introduce her to the Underground Railroad Quilt Story and the meaning of each square symbol.

Her inquisition led to a book that introduced quilters to this beautiful unknown story of how quilts were used as "directional signs" for the ones that traveled along to gain freedom in Canada.

At the time of the Underground Railroad, the entire quilt would bare just one symbol i.e. the basket, and this would prompt the slaves to look around for a covered basket filled with food.

These quilts hung on fences, clotheslines, in the yards of abolitionists. Mostly, made by slaves to help free slaves. Most people are not aware of this beautiful story and I'm certain that my Grandmother never knew the story.

Thus, my mother, 97, doesn't know this beautiful story but she just loves to make quilts of the symbols with her 92- and 86-year younger sisters. When I share the Underground Railroad Quilt Story with them; they simply say "Oh, well."

However, the story confirms that my people were crafty, swift, courageous, skillful, and hardworking. They knew how to be thankful for their God given blessings. One of my Grandmother's (Big Mama) quilts of the 'hole in the ground or cabin in the ground symbol' is displayed at the Alonzo A. Young, Sr. Enrichment & Historical Center in our historic Community Of Royal.

The quilt is tattered, worn and barely holding together. My Mom gifted it to me. Nevertheless, it's heartwarming just to know that it is stitched by my Big Mama's hands.

"Hello, Somebody!" Wake up and preserve your history that served the better good for humanity.

Story 6. How Do You Know Where You Are Going; If You Don't Know Where You Came From?

Steele introduces herself by sharing how growing up around such strong-willed people affected her life.

Now, for my introduction, I'll share a story that should explain the stock from which I came. One day when I was about 12 years old, my aunt, who was a great farming woman, asked my Mom/her sister if I could help in the field behind my house. Of course, my Mom didn't ask me and, of course, she agreed. Anything to help the farm survive, the farm was their livelihood. Off I was sent, out back to the field where the straightest rows of beautiful corn plants were growing.

Understand that I wasn't, and never thought of myself as a farm girl; I just lived on my family's 40-acre farm. If my Mom had asked me, I would have declined. My Mom! Ask me?! That wasn't happening.

The farm was just the backdrop for our house. Frankly, I wanted to be a business woman running a business - not farming.

I wanted to be as far away as I could get from the farm. Ironically though, my desire to become a business woman came from recognizing that my "Big Papa" was the owner of this beautiful farm. Therefore, my business, The Steele Organization, LLC is not named after me, but in honor of my "Big Papa."

I wasn't interested in working the farm; I was surprised that my aunt asked, and my Mom agreed. But anyhow, there I was standing in the field awaiting directions. Well, finally, my aunt said we're gonna put you on the tractor and you hold the steering wheel so that the tractor can stay on the straight and narrow path.

No, I didn't know how to drive- not even a car, especially not a tractor. Well, I climbed up on that tractor, which was fairly-new, and she hit the starter, put it in gear and told me to hold her straight down the row.

Turn left at the end of the row, then turn left into the next row, turn right at the end of that row, then turn right into the next row, then repeat until to the end of the rows.

This was a fairly-new tractor; this meant that it was used but new to us.

Okay, I thought this will not be so bad. I can hold her straight and I knew my right from my left. I was a straight A student, and this would be a piece of cake. I'll have my cake and eat it, too. So, slowly the tractor went, as I bounced up and down. I held on tight, steering straight down the rows of beautifully manicured rows. As a matter of fact, manicuring the rows was what my aunt and crew were doing. But they were one man short, and thus, I was on the tractor.

Everything was just great until Big Blackie, our 2000-pound Black Angus Bull, stepped out at the end of the row and began to graze.

Well, what is a little girl, all of approximately 75 pounds, to do with a 2000-pound bull who wasn't moving? All I knew was my aunt told me to hold the tractor

straight down the row and turn left, then turn left into the next row, turn right at the end of that row, then turn right into the next row. Then repeat until I reached the end of all rows.

She didn't mention anything about a 2000-pound bull. Also, I knew that I was on a fairly-new tractor and, for certain, Big Blackie was at the end of this row. I knew that if he didn't move, well, it would probably be bad for me and the tractor and not, necessarily so, for Big Blackie.

As the tractor drew closer to Big Blackie and my heart pounded even harder, my aunt stepped out facing down Big Blackie. In a stern voice, she said, "Blackie - move!" Blackie looked as if to say "are you talking to me?". Again, my aunt said with a little more sternness in her voice "Blackie - move! Blackie kept chewing as if to say "this grass is sweet, fresh and you want me to move? Not happening."

Now, it's a standoff and my aunt, with her sternest voice, said Blackie - move!" I guess one for the Father, one for the Son and one for the Holy Ghost as they always say in our church.

Well, Big Blackie continued to graze as if he was thinking, "Who does she think she's talking to?"

Of course, my aunt was talking to Blackie and continued her commands and walking towards him as if to say, "Who do you think you're ignoring?"

Big Blackie didn't move, as instructed. At that point, my aunt is standing directly in front of his face. She squared her body, grabbed him by the horns and twisted Blackie's 300+ pound head to the right and within seconds, the rest of his 1700-pound body went down to the ground.

All I could think was "my aunt- just flipped a 2000-pound Black Angus Bull! Don't mess with me!" Thus, my introduction: I am Beverly Steele, CEO of The Steele Organization, LLC, Founder of Young Performing Artists (YPAs), Inc., and niece of a woman who flipped a 2000-pound bull. I come from a long line of strong women. Women who could and would stand up to face any obstacles (bulls included); they used rocks as stepping-stones for and to success as well as believed in God, to boot. How do you know where you are going if you don't know where you came from?

"Hello, Somebody!" wake up to stand up.

Story 7. Reach for the Stars; If You Fall in the Clouds - It's Okay.

Royal's segregated Royal School closed at the end of the 1968-1969 school year. Steele recalls some of the fond memories, while attending her beloved community school, of the traditional and fundamental lessons she learned.

When I think of words to live by, I think of Mr. Alonzo A. Young, Sr. Mr. Young served as Principal, 22 years, of our dear segregated Royal School before it was closed due to mandatory integration. He was the last Principal of our Community School, which was renamed Royal Elementary & Middle School at its closure. "Mr. Young, Professor Young, Prof," were just a few of the dear names we called him.

He was more than our Principal; he was our cheerleader, our advocate, our motivator…. He didn't rule with an iron fist; he ruled with his "board of education" by his side. The board of education was a wooden plank about 2 feet long; ½ inch thick; 2 inches wide with a hand carved handle grip- probably, one of the men from the community set and whittled it from a board.

Yes, he had the parent's help and permission to use it whenever necessary "to put those hard headed 'young uns' in check; so they can learn something." And learn we did. No matter what learning ability or disability, we all learned the basics of the "3R's: **R**eading, W**R**iting and A**R**ithmetic."

As our advocate, he made certain that we had school books- they may have been hand-me-downs; but nevertheless, we had books. He fought hard for us to get the best 'used books' because he knew that we wouldn't get 'new' books. As our cheerleader, he challenged us to go for the good; whatever it was- go for it, "If it is good for you, our families, community, churches or the greater good." As our motivator, he would always say "Reach for the stars; if you fall in the clouds - it's okay."

I guess that's why this little farm girl never wanted to work the farm; I had, what I thought, higher aspirations. I wanted to be a Business Woman.

Yes, I worked on the farm. I worked during tobacco season as a tobacco handler every summer from the age of 13 to 19 until I moved away to attend Florida Agricultural & Mechanical University (FAMU), Tallahassee, Florida.

No, I didn't want to become a teacher. I wanted to be a business woman. No, I didn't want to become a nurse; a business woman. At that time, being a teacher or nurse was the acceptable careers for young African American girls. Don't get me wrong, those careers are fine choices. But not for me; I wanted to be a business woman - one who would pay it forward from the hard work, sweat and tears of my people that kept their land.

Paying it forward in my Big Papa's legacy. Did I think of it as Mr. Young described it? No, but I was shooting for my stars. I shot even higher, upon completing college. I was hired as a NYC business woman, truly a blessing. Then, I was further blessed to become a self-employed business woman owner - and remain so today.

Eventually, becoming the Founder of a statewide focused, not-for-profit business, providing services nationally and internationally.

With Mr. Young's and others' motivating words in my head; I have stayed the course! With my Big Papa's work ethics and good moral characteristics, I named my business in his honor. I heard the words from Mr. Young, but I saw the words take life through my grandfather's work on his 40-acre farm.

My grandfather, whose mother was full Cherokee, was a hardworking man for himself, his wife and his nine children. He never applied for, nor received a social security number because he never worked for anyone else. He knew he could own 40 acres; he achieved that because he reached for the stars and if he fell in the clouds, that was okay.

Yes, he did a little pickup work here and there, but he worked his land to provide for his family. He died at a fairly young age from lung cancer, he smoked heavily, probably a trait learned from his Cherokee side of the family.

When he was dying, he told his children to take care of Big Mama, take care of and keep the land. Thus, my aunt, worked that farm, all her life time, to keep the land.

I learned that when you work, sacrifice and reach for something whether it's stars(freedom); you can gain a soft landing in the clouds (40 acres). The Reverend Dr. Martin Luther King, Jr. stated in his speech (1967 Massey Lecture): "Deep in our history of struggle for freedom, Canada was the North Star - the star followed by the Underground Railroad. We sang of "heaven" that awaited us, and the slave masters listened in innocence, not realizing that we were not speaking of the hereafter. "Heaven" was the word for Canada/Freedom."

In the Underground Railroad Quilt Story, the boat symbol would denote which boat to board and make the trip to Canada/ Safety/ Freedom.

"Hello, Somebody!" Wake up and reach for the stars; if you fall in the clouds - it's okay if you are doing it for the 'greater good'.

Pictured: Royal Elementary & Middle School, circa 1969

Story 8. If you can't be the best; be among the best

During the 70s, major changes were happening. Steele shares how she transitioned- progression not regression - using her ancestor's principles.

1969-70 school year was the last school year offered at our dear Royal Elementary & Middle School. It was the last school year before mandatory integration and my class was the last 8th grade class to graduate from what started in 1874 as the Royal School. The Royal School evolved into Royal Elementary School and ending as the Royal Elementary & Middle School.

Mr. Alonzo A. Young, Sr. was the last sitting Principal completing 22 years. Mr. Young's impact on many lives was felt throughout many generations in our beloved community. For example, my brother, who was 18 years older than I, attended Royal school under Mr. Young; my Mom worked as one of the school's cooks under Mr. Young.

One of the school's traditions, passed from generation to generation, was Friday Assembly. A gathering of all parents, teachers, and community for the students to showcase what they had learned. Performances ranged from choirs singing to public speaking to May King & May Queen competitions to cheerleader selections, to sports Pep Rallies, etc.

Always, Mr. Young would give the last remarks. This format was very successful, because it was, and remains, the same format used in our community churches. Today and in my organization, we use this format at the close of our Youth Enrichment Programs.

As a child, it was comforting because it confirmed that the heart & soul of our community was established by the church and the school. This translated as, "you should always respect the church and the school. This further translated as "respect and listen to your leaders, elders and ancestors."

I remember, Mr. Young shared many sayings doing his remarks; some may be familiar as someone else's quotes. But, to us, they were Mr. Young's words of encouragement, motivation and enrichment. They were designed just for us. Only us! I wouldn't be surprised if Mr. Young shared others' quotes; he was well read and versed in many subjects. He was our highest-leveled educator in our community. He had more knowledge than our Pastors. He wasn't more important than our Pastors. Oh, no sir; no one was more important than the Men of God, our Pastors. Probably, he read and explained letters, reports, etc. for some of our Pastors but our churches were recognized as the leaders.

Nevertheless, Mr. Young would share words of wisdom at our school assemblies.

I remember this one that he would use more than once, "If you can't be the best; be among the best." As I write this quote, a question and answer just arose in my mind: Why didn't he just say, "Be the best or Be among the Best?"

The answer? I think it was because he became Principal in 1957 when separate was the normal and there was no equality. In his own career, it didn't matter if he was the best; he would never be recognized as the best. At that time, best wasn't described as the best of all; best was described as the best of the separate. He used wisdom with this saying; instead of saying, "you may never live to be recognized as the 'best;' even if you are the best. But, don't quit and accept being among the best." Mr. Young knew that if we didn't accept *it*; *it* would overcome us; *it* would overtake us; *it* would overshadow us. This reminds me of one of the songs we had to learn and sing at Royal's assembly: 'This Little Light Of Mine; I'm Gonna Let It Shine." Maybe, Mr. Young was saying if you are the best and among the best, someone will see your little, bright, shining light. What a great lesson to learn.

One of my favorite lessons learned was taught by one of my favorite Royal School teachers. The late great Ms. Almeda Walker. I believe that if she was alive and you ask her what was your greatest accomplishment as a teacher in Royal? She would answer "I made certain that my students knew how to spell and write their names." Ms. Walker spoke in a very nasal tone and she would say, under her breath, "You won't go through life signing an X; you will learn how to spell and write your name."

She was a taskmaster and would walk the room with her ruler to "crack your knuckles" until you held your pencil correctly; make that letter correctly and place the letters to spell your name correctly.

I can just imagine how important this was to Ms. Walker. Most likely, she held the highest education in her immediate and extended family of aunts, uncles, and cousins. Probably, it was her responsibility to read every document; fill out every voter's registration form; complete every government required form, etc. just to have her people sign their understanding with just an acceptable X.

She had learned to be more than an X; she wanted us to become more than an X. This wasn't such an easy task because of students like my late brother. My dad was one of Royal's big farmers and my brother thought that he was just as good as my Dad. In his mind, he was the best farmer at that Royal school and he didn't need school; he knew how to farm.

He wasn't afraid of Ms. Walker's "knuckle cracker;". All others were; we were completely quiet and focused during her class. Well for my brother it was just too much quietness for a farmer; he would just blurt out cow noises- "MOO, MOO." Of course, the entire class would laugh.

Ms. Walker, in her eloquent but nasal tone, would call him by his name and say, "you are not a cow, stop making cow noises and get back to your work." Which he didn't, because to my brother, farming was his work, not this reading, writing and arithmetic stuff. He wasn't the best studied but nevertheless, he never signed an X; he signed his first, middle and last name. Job well done, Ms. Walker.

If you can't be the best; be among the best. This moved with me from my beloved Royal school to my beloved Wildwood High School (WHS). As I previously stated, my 8th grade class was the last graduating class from our Royal school. I didn't graduate with this class because I was transferred to WHS (the white school). I will never forget the day my Mom and I went to our family doctor for my school physical. His office was familiar to me; I had visited at least twice during my 7th grade year because of bronchial infections. I was small frame and asthmatic as a young child. Those were two of the times that my Mom had to seek medical help.

Other times we used home remedies that worked, but not those two times. This time, I needed a school physical examination by the same doctor that treated my two bronchial infections.

I remember as if it was yesterday. At the end of my examination, my doctor turned to face my Mom, and with a straight face, stated that I had passed my physical. Then he added, "however, she is low on iron, which I will continue to treat, but she passed her physical."

As he continued, he called my Mom by her name and asked if she planned to re-enroll me in the Royal School. He stated, "I asked because if you intend to send her back to the Royal School; I will call the authorities. He stated that he heard this was the last year this school would be open. He knew they were planning to close the school. Also, he knew they wouldn't put money into the necessary repairs needed i.e. repairing the heating.

He continued by stating that the heating was inadequate and that caused my bronchial infections. I don't think her little body, which has always been prone to asthma, can take many more episodes of bronchial infections. The heating will not be upgraded, and you need to move her this school year. With the history dating back to 1874, my Mom really didn't want to move me because this was our beloved school.

Calling my Mom by her name, once again, he stated, "It's your decision as a Parent, but if you bring her back and she has another bronchial infection; I will call the authorities."

I remember that my Mom didn't answer a yeah or nay; she heard the words, understood the words, received the prescription, paid our bill and we left.

Now, I'm realizing what a profound moment this was in my life. Not, because of the threat the Doc mentioned, but because of how my Mom handled the threat. She offered the threat giver no power in her decision; she left the threat giver not knowing if the threat was taken or rejected.

She understood the value of life to him as a doctor. Also, she understood the value of making her own decisions as an African American woman. Yes, she valued my life, as well and she moved me. But in that moment, her reaction was a valuable life lesson for me. I used this same tactic when one of my NYC upper level manager threatened me.

I received my first invitation to sit as a Board of Director member; I was advised that it would be wise to get my manager's permission. I clearly didn't agree, and my confidant said, "If you want to be seen as a team player - you should."

Finally, I, reluctantly, agreed. When the moment arrived; I told (not asked) my manager. He leaned back in his chair and said, "Oh, you were?'"

He continued, "I'm wondering why they asked you and not me? I don't understand. In that case, my answer would have to be 'No,' I don't approve." I remember thinking this is my first invite as a BOD member. This was a group that was discussing the issues surrounding minority youth in minority communities and neighborhoods and he's wondering why they didn't invite him?

I picked up my writing tablet, my pen and I said, "Thank you." The next day, I called and accepted the position. It was at that board table that I met African Americans who helped me start my business: a lawyer and an accountant. "Thanks, Mom!"

I remember another life moment where I applied Mr. Young's words; it was the move to the "white school." Before the move, my Mom met with Mr. Young to share her decision to move me.

This is when I first learned of the move; my Mom didn't ask me what I wanted to do as some parents do today. She was the parent that provided; I was the child that received the provisions. I had to listened to her; she had my best interest at heart. She didn't have to listen to me. I was a child; I didn't know what best interest to hold dear to my heart.

Mr. Young truly understood. He called my Mom by her name stating, "I hate to lose her; I hate to admit that the Doc is right; I will make certain that she continues to learn at the high level of learning that she has demonstrated."

He knew that I was 1st or 2nd in my class throughout my Royal School years. One of my cousins and I were the same age. Between us, our class ranking fluctuated from 1st to 2nd every year. For example, she had the highest grade at the end of our first grade; I had the second highest.

For second grade, I had the highest and she the second, and for the third, she was the highest and I was second, and so, on and on. Therefore, in our eighth grade, maybe destiny would have prevailed once again, and I could have risen to the top.

We'll never know because of the move. Mr. Young was assuring my Mom that he would do his best to circumvent me being placed in remedial classes - just because of who I am. The next week, we met Mr. Young while grocery shopping. He told my Mom that he had spoken with the Assistant Principal and advised him that I was coming to his school. He apprised him of my GPA and told him to look out for one of his "star students." Mr. Young told my Mom, "When you take her to register, stop by the office, ask for the Assistant Principal before you start the process. Don't forget that," he asserted.

After working a 6am – 2pm shift, my Mom and I went to register. We went to the office, asked for the Assistant Principal. He was the first African American Assistant Principal in the County.

The desk clerk delayed announcing us and allowed others to go before us to meet with him. When my Mom inquired, she was told that she didn't have to wait for him; you can go to so and so building to register. My Mom was tired - too tired to play games. We went to register me; we received my schedule.

When we passed the office and were almost off campus, we heard the Assistant Principal's booming voice calling out. He knew us, from the community, shopping, church, etc. At that time, schools were still being managed by community folks instead of what's happening in schools- today. After greeting us, he asked to see my schedule. Yep, just like Mr. Young predicted, all my classes were remedial classes.

He asked the classic question: "Is this her schedule?" "Yes," my Mom answered. "Did they look at her transcript?" "No," Mom responded. He took us back to his office where he made a phone call to the registration team; asked a series of questions, then asked if my Mom would allow him to re-address my schedule.

"Yes." He escorted us back to so and so building; I took a test; passed the test and was placed in "Prep courses" which are now known as "honor courses." In twelfth grade, I graduated fifth out of the 100 students in my class.

That was my 8th grade and five years later, I began college. Once again, I was surprised when I was escorted by a top administrator back to registration because of the same reasons. I was placed in remedial college-level course studies. This time, it wasn't an Assistant Principal - it was the President!

Can you imagine what it felt like to this 18-year-old? I was put out of my class because I was answering the simple math questions before the Professor could finish asking. The Math Professor asked, 'what's the highest level of math that I had taken?'. "Trigonometry", I replied. He, promptly, stepped into his office; made a phone call; stepped out of his office; told me to get my books and go to the President's office.

I thought that was bad but that wasn't as bad as an 18-year-old having the President walk you across the campus, carrying your books while everyone is looking and thinking, "What on earth did Beverly do?" Not only were they thinking it; Beverly was thinking the same thing! I knew I had done nothing, but it felt like I did something.

Yes, five years later, the College President had to ensure that I was registered according to my transcript (my work). I was surprised because I thought things (race relations) were better. We had lived through the riots; made interracial friendships; accepted the first African Americans in many different areas within our schools, work places, communities, etc. Did we? Or, didn't we?

Speaking in April 1865, Frederick Douglas said, "Everybody has asked, 'What shall we do with the Negro?' I have but one answer. Do nothing with us! All I ask is, give him a chance. If you see him on his way to school, let him alone.

If you see him going to the dinner-table at a hotel, let him go! If you see him going to the ballot-box, don't disturb him. If you see him going into a workshop, just let him alone. If you will only un-tie his hands and give him a chance, I think he will live."

"Hello, Somebody!" Wake up; Live your best life and let others live theirs.

If you can't be the best; be among the best.

Story 9. Be Kind, Be Humble, Love Your Neighbor and Serve God

---

Steele moved back to Royal and was running her business when she had a change of heart about business. She moved in a different direction and it has made all the difference.

My Mom shared many words throughout my lifetime, i.e. "Be kind, be humble, love your neighbor, and serve God." Those were the ones that my Big Mama shared with her, and she passed on to us.

"Be kind, be humble, love your neighbor and serve God" are the words that must have been the motivator when I founded my beloved not-for-profit, 501 c)3), statewide focused, state recognized corporation: "Young Performing Artists (YPAs), Inc."

In 1998, I had moved back to Royal for six years; focused on running my for-profit business: "The Steele Organization (TSO), LLC." My thoughts were how to maintain my business, especially now that I was back in Royal where my vision began. I had traveled and spoke of, how my business was an honor to my Big Papa.

This statement took on a new meaning in Royal; I realized that having my business live up to his standards was a real test because the people knew my Big Papa's standards.

I was busy ensuring that my for-profit business lived up to pay honor to his legacy. I was not thinking about starting a not-for-profit business. As a matter of fact, I never wanted to work for, manage or have anything to do with or for a not-for-profit business - except to make donations.

It was 1986, when I made this vow while enjoying dinner with friends. One of my friends was Marketing Director for a national not-for-profit corporation. When the bill arrived, it was my turn to pick up the tab; I put down my card. Of course, when the waiter returned, he/she brought a pen for signing. This pen was not my "Cross" gold pen; I quickly tossed it to the side and retrieved my Cross. As the rejected pen fell to the side, my girlfriend asked, "Does anyone want that pen?"

Well, we all were NYC Corporate Managers, had worked hard, survived many obstacles to gain our Cross pens and we promptly stated, "No, we have our own special pens." Ms. Marketing Director stated, "So do I, but I'm in the not-for-profit industry. I'm at the end of my quarterly budget, and I need pens." At that point, we emptied our purses. All our rejected pens, at the bottom of our purses, were placed on the table because our girlfriend needed help. I vowed, that I would never work for, manage or have anything to do with a not-for-profit, except donate. My Cross pen was ordered by my for-profit company. It looked good and felt good, as well.

Then life happened in 1991, my firm was hired to travel to Portland, Oregon to discuss Equity & Diversity in the workplace. After the discussion, I ventured outside to enjoy the downtown Portland area where I met a young artist sitting on a park bench.

He was perplexed about life. After greetings and a series of concerned questions, he opened up and began to share. He was a high school senior and couldn't understand why his friends who wanted to work with computers; or work as a nurse or doctor; or as a teacher; or as a business person, had so many opportunities (monies) to further their futures in those fields.

He asked, 'why this isn't available in "the Arts?" I knew he was an artist; I have always had an innate sense of artistic characteristics in a person. In other words, I can spot an artist a mile away, especially young artists.

I didn't have an answer until 1997 when I, for the first time, made a profit from my business. A strong voice spoke to my soul, "Start a not-for-profit." I asked my soul, "Who me? You must have the wrong soul because I vowed, that I would never work for, manage or have anything to do with a not-for-profit - except donate." I continued, "Soul, don't you know that? You should know that by now."

Apparently, my soul didn't listen because I began the necessary paperwork. I asked, "Soul, what's the name?" It answered, "Young Performing Artists," and I asked "Of Royal? Or Sumter County? Or What?"

My soul responded with, "Don't forget the young man in Oregon." At that point, I reached for the stars and felt my soul agree to a statewide focus with a national and international appeal.

Now, I was perplexed. How can a little girl from Royal ever phantom such a thing? Then, I remembered my Mom's words, "Be kind, be humble, love your neighbor and serve God." I don't remember the young man's name, but I pray that he remembered that I told him, "No matter what career you have to choose; the arts chose you. Do what you have to do, but never forget your art."

I didn't promise to start an organization that would help address his concern because I vowed, that I would never work for, manage or have anything to do with a not-for-profit - except donate." The understanding, meaning and purpose of words passed down by my ancestors and forefathers were somehow clouded by a gold pen. Nothing is wrong with having a gold pen or a special anything, but now I understand why my soul persisted. Those words, that were implanted early in my spirit, had to be awakened.

Judges 5: 12-13 reads: "Awake, awake, Deborah: awake, awake, utter a song: arise, Barak, and lead thy captivity captive, thou son of Abinoam. Then he made him that remaineth have dominion over the nobles among the people: the Lord made me have dominion over the mighty."

"Hello, Somebody!" Wake up! Be kind, be humble, love your neighbor and serve God.

Story 10. Six in One Hand; Half a Dozen in the Other. There's More Than One Way to Skin a Cat.

With the good characteristics of her people embedded in her soul, Steele felt well equipped to face her own future.

While working in NYC, I visited home frequently. Each time, my Big Mama would summons me for a "talk." She would always start with the question, "Did you get married, yet? Are you thinking of marriage? Are you dating?" Promptly, I reminded her that I'm her granddaughter who never intended to marry nor have any children. She would say, "Never say never!" She always had more words of wisdom.

I would quickly move the conversation to another subject – maybe a situation from my childhood that I wasn't quite clear as to why it happened. For example, I remember asking her 'why my aunt picked me to work in the tobacco crop?'. I grew up on the farm, lived and played around the farm, but I wasn't a "farm girl." So, why my aunt would pick me to work tobacco was always a mystery to me.

My job was "Tobacco Handler." I would hand a measured amount of tobacco leaves to my aunt; she would take a string and tie the leaves onto the tobacco stick. The loaded sticks were hung in the barn to dry out. I became known as a good "Tobacco Handler" but I handed the tobacco to my youngest aunt, who was known as the best "Tobacco Stringer".

That was a true art and a decade old process that helped make all the gathering of the plants; tilling of the soil; planting of the plants; cultivating the plants, and harvesting the plants a success. The success was when my Big Papa and the men of the community would go to the market and returned with pockets full of money.

So, we thought. Sometimes, the buyers would "steal" our tobacco; they would claim that the tobacco wasn't "good cigarette quality"--- it was "good for nothing" --- and paid them "good for nothing" quality rate.

My people knew that the buyers would take that same tobacco and use it for cigars. "Cigar quality" paid at a higher rate than "cigarette quality" tobacco. My people knew that they wouldn't get cigar quality rates even if their tobacco was; they just claimed it was "good for nothing." The men would return disappointed in the system but thankful for their part in the process.

This particular talk with Big Mama led to her wise words about the process. As I pondered and waited for her answer to why me? She simply stated, "You had to learn how to work; how to make a living to take care of your family. You learned how to do that as a tobacco handler. Didn't you?" Again, I reminded her that I wasn't planning on having a family, nor a farm. She said, "Well then, you had to learn how to work and take care of you!"

I said, "But I don't do that kind of work; that's why I worked hard to obtain a college degree." "Yes, that's right you worked hard," she said.

“That’s the point- you worked hard. You learned how to work hard for that degree and now you have a nice job in NYC from learning how to work hard when you were a tobacco handler. Tobacco handler was one of the jobs we could offer because we are farmers. We had farming jobs to help you learn how to work hard.”

She continued, “The point is, Baby, six in one hand; a half dozen in the other. There’s more than one way to skin a cat. It’s in the way/ the process. You had to learn to wrap your mind, heart and soul around the way/ the process to do it and do it right.

You see, Baby, you can find your way to six simply by going to six. Or you can take a dozen, then divide it in half to find your way to six. More than one way/ process to skin a cat. If someone tries to stop one way; try another but keep going until that cat is skinned (mission accomplished).”

“Baby, you worked hard at handing that tobacco and you were one of the best in the area. You worked just as hard at your school lessons; getting all those A’s and completing high school with honors. Then, off to college.

You did the same thing, getting all those A's and graduating with honors. Now, you have a career that fits your degree. You learned to work hard as a tobacco handler, the one job that we had to offer. You had to learn the process, the way of working hard to survive in life."

Your Aunt offered what we had, a farming job. It looks like our farming job paid off. Now, "why aren't you married, yet? Why aren't you thinking of marring? Not even- dating?" I replied, "Oh, Big Mama, I'll be alright."

"Hello, Somebody!" Wake up! It's all in the ways (processes) you can use to skin that cat.

Story 11. Baby Don't Sell Your Soul; For God Owns It and the Devil Wants To Buy It.

Steele shares how talking with Big Mama, while working in the corporate world in the 70's & 80's, was enlightening. A profound moment; Steele realized that Big Mama understood the challenges of her world even though Big Mama never worked in Steele's world.

Another profound moment as I traveled the roads of my life; I was visiting home and, as usual, talking with Big Mama. After her first question: "Are you married, yet?" was answered with a resounding, "NO," she asked, "How is work?"

It was the late 70s, early 80s and I was a first level management employee with my first major New York City corporation. I shared with Big Mama that I had just completed my first major department meeting. She said, "That sounds good; how did that go?" I said, "It went well, very well." She replied, with eyebrows lifted, "Oh! No problems?" I replied, "Big Mama; It went well, very well but there was this one guy who tried to trip me up."

She said, with brows lifted, "What happened!" I shared that there was a young man, who was the relative of one of the company's top executives and he was an Ivy League College grad. He gave everyone the business.

He didn't agree with anything; he was condescending; he mentioned his degree, repeatedly; he was disrespectful; he was just obnoxious ... which was how most others described him. She said, "What did he do to you?"

Well, I was new to the company and to that department. My manager had given me an assignment from day one that I worked on, found a solution and was working to resolve. My manager thought it was a good idea for me to present my results at this meeting. Other managers had expressed a similar situation that they were also trying to solve. After my presentation, all were very complementary and surprised that I was using a relatively simple solution to resolve this department-wide problem.

They looked around the room at others, in my position, for their feedback. Most stated that they were very busy with other priorities; thanked me for my work and they really wanted to hear the outcomes. This was slowly becoming a priority especially since it was something left unaddressed.

Well, "Mr. Ivy League grad" didn't like that at all. He began attacking how simple the solution was and he wasn't surprised because of where I had earned my degree. I am a Historically Black College & University (HBCU) grad. He continued by using "big vocabulary words," as if I didn't know their meaning and added, "If you know what I mean?" Others stated that, as he asked, he was looking directly at me. I wasn't looking at him and had no intentions of looking at him; I would have given him a piece of my mind. AND, if I had put my hands on my hips like my Big Mama when she set you straight; it wouldn't have been pleasant.

In other words, he was stating that my solution was too simple to come from him - an Ivy League grad.

I just stated that I would share the results with whomever was interested. My manager began to speak, but his manager broke my manager's dialogue stating "I don't care how simple. It's working; that's what matters." Then, his manager assigned him to check with me for the process and implement it in their department. Two weeks later, he resigned.

Immediately after the meeting, everyone I talked with or called me stated, "Congratulations; you handled that very well. You also solved a problem that we all know existed but didn't want to tackle." I said, "Big Mama, can you believe he tried me in front of everyone." She said, "I'm very proud of you for not giving him a piece of your mind. It wasn't worth it." Then she said, "Remember, Baby, don't sell your soul because God owns it, and the Devil wants to buy it."

He didn't know who I was because I hadn't learned who I was. I was born in the "lily-white hospital" because my Big Papa had acquired the first insurance that he could purchase.

The "lily-white insurance" could only be used at "lily-white hospitals". The nearest hospital was in Tampa, Florida. He didn't know that my Mom had borne that hour-long trip, twice, to give birth. Mr. Ivy League grad didn't know that I had an aunt who flipped a 2000-pound bull. He didn't know that my education started at the Royal Elementary & Middle School, a segregated school with little resources. I graduated with Honors.

He didn't know that in 8th grade I went to the integrated school and experienced my first taste of the integrated but separate movement. He didn't know that even though I was an honor student at my segregated school, they placed me in remedial classes at the integrated school. He didn't know that the first African American Assistant Principal, in that integrated environment, had to personally oversee my registration. He had to ensure that I was given the Prep-Course test to be accepted as a "Prep" student.

He didn't know that I had the 3rd highest score on that 'Prep' test. He didn't know that I had survived the riots, the walk outs, the protest, to graduate with honors- 5th in my class of 100.

He didn't know that the cycle repeated itself when I enrolled, for one year, at my local Community College. Once again, even though I was an honor student, I was placed in remedial classes.

He didn't know that the first day of college, my Math Professor put me out of his class; sent me to the President's office. This was after he contacted admissions and there was no resolve to his question of "why this girl, who took Trigonometry, is in my remedial math class?".

He didn't know that the President, personally, escorted me back through admissions, changed my schedule and escorted me to the new class that was already in session to explain. He didn't know that at FAMU, I was a work-study student who graduated on the Dean's list; the #1 student in my department and with honors.

He didn't know that I was a direct descendant of one of the founding families of our historic Community of Royal. My Big Mama was one of their daughters.

He just didn't know, that all I had been through, I wasn't selling my soul; because God owns it and the Devil wants to buy it.

"Hello, Somebody!" Wake up! Stop judging the book by its cover.

Story 12. Put Extra to Your Ordinary

In today's world, Steele prays that her people will realize, never forget, and respect stories of their heritage.

Several years after founding my organization, I received several media interview opportunities. One opportunity was when a magazine reporter called to include me in their upcoming annual "Women Issue." He apologized for the lateness and not being able to visit for a face- to-face talk. But, he certainly wanted to include me as one of the business women of the area.

I said, to myself, "Self, if you were really considered as one of the business women of the area you would have been one of the first called." What, probably, happened was after completing the article, they realized that it wasn't a good reflection of the women business owners of the area.

I thought to myself, nevertheless, you were asked.

He preceded to ask questions: the Whys, the Hows, the Whats, etc. As the last question, he asked me to "pick a word that best described me,". Immediately, I said, "Extraordinary," which shocked me as the word fell out of my mouth. He asked, "Why that word?" As shocked as I was about the word that fell out; I was equally or more shocked that I said "because I put extra to my ordinary".

At that time, I shouldn't have been shocked because we had begun the process of developing my organization's local project: Royal Historical Enrichment & Art Program (RHEAP). RHEAP because we are reaping the harvest from our Fore Fore Forefathers and mothers as well as our own hard work.

RHEAP is a historical, culturally based, art enhanced, enriching program with two components: historical and enrichment.

The historical component is mostly about the rich and beautiful Community of Royal's history.

By this time, I had gained knowledge of "my people" who had put extra to their ordinary to gain their 40 acres after the Civil War; held onto the land after President Abraham Lincoln's assassination, and pass the land down through their generations. This was despite the "night riders" ravaging the crops and livestock in order to retake the land. Yet, my people kept their land.

Today, my prayer is that my people realize, never forget, respect and share the stories of the "extra" that our Fore Forefathers and mothers placed on their "ordinary." Ordinary, for them, was slavery without ownership. Then, freedom with ownership, January 1865. Then, freedom without ownership, June 1865.

Doesn't ownership lead to freedom? Isn't that the American way? It's disturbing that there is so much dialogue regarding whether my people should have or shouldn't have been in slavery for 200+ years; whether they choose to or were forced. Those, who are questioning, are some of my own people; including the younger ones who have gained because of the extra that our people placed on their ordinary.

I'm concerned. I'm quite confident that they are aware that their gain was achieved because of the extra that our people placed to their ordinary. For example, Frederick Douglass, who risked offending others, addressed 500 Abolitionists at the invitation of the Ladies Anti-Slavery Society at Corinthian Hall, July 5, 1852 in Rochester, New York, a city known for its abolitionist activities.

He delivered one of his most powerful speeches: "What to the Negro Is the Fourth of July?" The first part of his speech praises our country's founding fathers and it finishes questioning slavery. Yes, I would imagine that Mr. Douglass was nervous before, during and after his speech but he placed the extra to his ordinary because he knew there had to be an awakening of the mindset.

Today, I'm concerned about the younger generation not realizing, forgetting, not respecting and not sharing their stories with their generations; our future.

When I look at the evolution of my people, beginning (pre-Civil War) with slavery without ownership (ownership equaled financial stability); to freedom (end of Civil War) with ownership (ownership equaled financial stability); to freedom (during reconstruction) without ownership (ownership equaled financial stability) and back to freedom (post-Civil Rights movement) with ownership (ownership equaled financial stability).

My concern is how can the younger ones ask why and how enslavement lasted for 200+ years? Maybe, the question should be does ownership equal financial stability for people?

My question to them is simple, "Have you done or are you doing what our forefathers, foremothers, abolitionists and others did to help move the freedom process along?"

When I started my first business partnership, we met with the President of a major corporation in New York City. My partner, another African American female, and I introduced him to a new marketing concept.

The President was so impressed that we knew someone who wasn't afraid to ask him to grant us a meeting. He stated how impressed he was that we knew this person; he was impressed with how we spoke, our intelligence, our good concepts, but he had one question: "Why are you here? Why are you here asking me, when there are so many African Americans sports figures, entertainers, etc., who can help their own people?" He continued, "If you ladies can get in my chairs? Why can't you get into theirs? Why are you here asking me?"

My answer was, "ones who look like us can't get to them because they are surrounded by ones who look like you." I responded that way because it was true. Of course, I realized that he didn't need us; we needed him. He loved our idea of "Brand marketing" by using some of the African American superstars, i.e. sportsman, singers, actors, etc., to promote his products. I knew he could execute it without us, but I had to speak the truth.

I had to 'wake him up'. I don't know why but I had to. And, they did execute without us; I don't know if it opened doors for Queen Latifah, Rhianna, Halle Barry, etc., but I do know that it wasn't happening before we met with this President. I spoke the truth.

Unfortunately, this holds true today. The time was early 1980's. I have never forgotten that "profound moment." I never will because I still must travel that same road today. That is what is disconcerting! I'm not challenging, who you marry, how you make your money or where you choose to live. Nor, what you think about slavery because what you think - is an opinion.

My opinion is that slavery happened; it's written in the Lamb Book Of Life (in my Big Mama's words). It's history that needs to be realized, never forgotten, respected and shared because of the extra that people placed to their ordinary. I've learned the who, what, why and how about myself from those shared stories.

My concern is that in 2019, I'm still traveling the same road – pattern - process for advancement. For our countywide African American History Month program, we presented the Florida Humanities Council's program entitled "Ersula Odom's in-character performance of Dr. Mary McLeod Bethune Comes To Life." While sitting there, I realized that the same resources that Dr. Bethune used were the same as I use today. It was unsettling because Dr. Bethune had limited resources; there wasn't many of her people that she could approach. Today, it's not the same limited resources - but the same limited access.

I am so thankful for all our supporters, as was the late Dr. Bethune. Once they heard; they believed and supported. I am thankful as well as Dr. Bethune. My further concern is that my people, who are privileged or blessed to grow up with money, or as my Big Mama would say "with a silver lining or a silver spoon in their mouth," will they learn how to do it differently?

Or, will this cycle continue? Will they teach their children? Or, will this cycle continue? "When you learn, teach", Maya Angelou. I will add, with my brows raised as did Big Mama, "if you learn 'nothing' then you teach 'nothing'."

My Mom said that my Big Mama, told her to "Reach out your hands; have something in them that people can take out to help themselves. If they place something in your extended hands, it will be on top of what you have. That you can work and grow. Then, I can reach my hands out again; and the process will repeat itself." Reconstruction simply means to build anew.

"Hello, Somebody!" Wake Up! Let's place the extra to our ordinary; it's very much needed to make a real change.

Last Thoughts: What is it about family that matters to God?

Steele, who is often invited as a Guest Speaker, shares her speech delivered at her 2018 family reunion Sunday Worship service. Steele shares and prays that her family will realize, never forget, and respect stories of their heritage.

What is it about family that matters to God?
Anderson, Robinson, Steele Family Reunion
August 19, 2018

What is it about family that matters to God? Thou shalt have no other gods before me.

Exodus 20:1-6
And God spake all these words, saying, I am the LORD thy God, which have brought thee out of the land of Egypt, out of the house of bondage.
Thou shalt have no other gods before me. Thou shalt not make unto thee any graven image, or any likeness of anything that is in heaven above, or that is in the earth beneath, or that is in the water under the earth:

Thou shalt not bow down thyself to them, nor serve them: for I the LORD thy God am a jealous God, visiting the iniquity of the fathers upon the children unto the third and fourth generation of them that hate me; And shewing mercy unto thousands of them that love me, and keep my commandments.

1-3 God said to tell the family that what matters to me, your LORD thy God, which have brought thee out of the land of Egypt, out of the house of bondage. Thou shalt have no other gods before me. In other words, He brought our Forefathers and mothers out of the land of slavery; out of the house of having no rights to having rights; out of not allowed to own land and possessions to owning land and possessions to help not only ourselves but to help our people.

What is it about family that matters to God? Thou shalt have no other gods before me.

In other words, He's asking why are we raising our children unlike our ancestors - unlike His principles? Where in Psalms 34:11- it reads- Come, ye children, hearken unto me: I will teach you the fear of the LORD.

God said ask the family why are we raising our children to believe that if we don't give you a birthday party from age one then we don't love you? He said your ancestors didn't do this - they taught you the fear of the Lord. God said ask the family why are we teaching our children that we can't go to church if we don't have all matching outfits; if we don't have the latest style shoes; if we don't have the latest style clothing; if our hair is wiped, flipped, tossed and dyed; if we can't take a picture to place on Facebook, Twitter, Instagram, Social Media?

What is it about family that matters to God? Thou shalt have no other gods before me.

God said remind your Family, that your ancestors helped build this church and community to ensure that His word lives on. NO, they were not sinless, and neither are we; but they had no other gods before Him. Now that you know this, God said ask your family why do we allow our children to emulate others, who we don't know what their beliefs are, instead of emulating your own ancestors?

In other words, why are we having 'Baby Bump Photo Shoots' for our unwed 13, 14, 15, 16, 17, 18, 19-year-old young Mothers. No, you don't have to teach them to be ashamed of their mistake but what's up with that?

What is it about family that matters to God? Thou shalt have no other gods before me.

God said ask your family – 'whose family values matter?' Your ancestors, who I brought out of slavery, or the values of the latest 'Reality Show' family? In other words, He brought our Forefathers and mothers out of the land of slavery; out of the house of having no rights to having rights; out of not allowed to own land and possessions to owning land and possessions to help not only ourselves but to help our people instead, we build our lives around what we see the latest 'Reality Show' family and/or wives are doing. What's up with that?

What is it about family that matters to God? Thou shalt have no other gods before me.

"Hello, Somebody!" Wake Up!

References & Bibliography

Lighting the Fires of Freedom, African American Women In The Civil Rights Movement. Janet Dewart Bell. The New Press. New York. London.

Digital Heritage Interactive, LLC- González-Tennant, Edward 2017- Community Of Royal Cultural Resources Assessment Survey. Florida Division of Historical Resources Archives. Florida Department of State.

Dr. Donald Paul Wyman, Author. "The Chosen Path: Based on the Life of Elizabeth Van Lew; Member of The Villages Civil War Study Group; Florida.

Forty Acres & Maybe A Mule. Harriette Gillem Robinet. Wendell Minor, Illustrator. Aladdin Paperbacks. New York, New York.

González-Tennant, Edward 2016 Hate Sits in Places: Folk Knowledge and the Power of Place in Rosewood, Florida. In Excavating Memory: Material Culture Approaches to Sites of Remembering and Forgetting, edited by Maria T. Starzmann and John R. Roby, pp. 218-241. Gainesville: University Press of Florida

Howard, Rosalyn 2013 "Looking for Angola": An Archaeological and Ethnohistorical Search for a Nineteenth Century Florida Maroon Community and its Caribbean Connections. The Florida Historical Quarterly 92(1): 32-68.

Howard, Rosalyn 2002 Black Seminoles in the Bahamas. Gainesville: University Press of Florida.

Ingram, Sonja. 2015 Pittsylvania County Tobacco Barn Survey: Final Report. Richmond: Preservation Virginia.

Nichols, Hulon H. 2002 Long Hammock Memories. St. Petersburg: Ideal Publishing Co., Inc.

The Trouble They Seen. The Story of Reconstruction, In the words of African Americans. Edited by Dorothy Sterling. Da Capo Press. New York.

Underground Railroad Sampler. Eleanor Burns. Sue Bouchard. Quilt In A Day Publisher.

FROM THE AUTHOR…………

In writing this book, my focus was to recall my people stories and give them a voice in telling their own stories. Being very careful, to ensure, that their oral stories are well respected and represented.

For these oral histories are the real witness to the Reconstruction era. These stories should become the true historical accounts to capture the heart, spirit and soul of an integral part of the 'whole' American historical picture.

For with these stories, we can better understand that sector of people and their culture. Making us knowledgeable; less judgmental and more tolerable of each other.

For without these stories, some may judge an entire race unfavorable without any substantiating evident.

A lot of my stories are the actions of the women in my life. This reminds me of Roger Hickey's, Co-Director, Campaign for America's Future, and he said "African American Women challenged and broke the system of Jim Crow and segregation- and in the process, inspired and helped to lead the women's movement. These incredible women were 'woke' before anyone ever used that word."

I pray that my people stories are vital to creating better humanities of the threads that's intertwined in the fabrics of the American quilt. I desire to use these stories to connect us to where we came from while being rooted in where we are.

"Hello, Somebody!"

Beverly Steele is the CEO and Owner of The Steele Organization, LLC a for profit Marketing & Management Consulting firm. Also, Steele is the Founder of Young Performing Artists, Inc. a 501 c) 3) not for profit, statewide focused, state corporation.

Steele is the recipient of the Robert W. Saunders' Library's Lamp of Knowledge Award, the Daughters of the Union 1861-1865 Civil War Remembrance Award, the Florida Alliance for Arts Education Business Leader Statewide award, the Sumter County Community Hero award, and a 2015 WEDUTV Be More Entrepreneurial Finalist. She has a Bachelor of Science with a Minor in Business Administration from Florida A & M University. She lives in the Community Of Royal with her husband and her 97-year young Mom.

Made in the USA
Columbia, SC
28 July 2024

39462571R00062